Pigs ina Poke™
Collection #2

Pigs ina Poke™

Collection #2

D. A. Hammond

with satirical prose by
Lawrence K. DeLamarter and Bradley Marion

Beech River Books

Center Ossipee, N.H.

BRB
Beech River Books
P.O. Box 62, Center Ossipee, N.H. 03814
1-603-539-3537
www.beechriverbooks.com

First edition

LIBRARY OF CONGRESS CATALOGING-IN-PUBLICATION DATA

Hammond, D. A. (Duane A.)
    Pigs ina poke, collection #2 / D.A. Hammond ; with satirical prose by Lawrence K. DeLamarter and Bradley Marion. -- 1st ed.
        p. cm.
    Summary: "Artwork and accompanying text depicting pigs in whimsical and satirical human situations"--Provided by publisher.
    ISBN 978-0-9793778-8-4 (pbk. : alk. paper) 1. Hammond, D. A. (Duane A.) 2. Swine in art. 3. Swine--Humor. 4. Puns and punning. I. DeLamarter, Lawrence K. II. Marion, Bradley. III. Title. IV. Title: Pigs in a poke, collection #2. V. Title: Pigs ina poke, collection no. 2.
    NC139.H255A4 2010
    741.5'6973--dc22

                            2010035446

Printed in China

To Donna, Lorrie and Brian, offsprings
of my wife Sandy and me, who if they were pigs,
would all be blue ribbon winners.

Table of Contents

Hear, See, Squeal No Evil

Foreword

To the best of my knowledge, Duane Hammond is the only artist creating fine art pig paintings, illustrating hilarious satire using pigs as the subjects. After having a very successful first book of pigs with whimsical titles, he has created his second book which will tickle your funny bone. Duane is a friend, fellow author, and humorist for all of the years I have known him. Every time we meet he always has some quip of humor about life's circumstances. Duane is a master of preposterous wit....Take a look at titles such as: Salt Pork, Hoggis MacDuff, Powder Pig, and Bacon in the Sun. Be prepared to do a great deal of laughing, so warn anyone standing around you about what you are going to do.

—Joe Smiga, author of *Behind The Lies*

Introduction

When is the last time you heard someone laughing in an art museum?

Art should evoke a response from the viewer. As we walk through a gallery or exhibit, we are moved by the subject, color and rendition of the work and might feel awed, uplifted, anguished or shamed by what we observe. I hope the art world can also accept humor and that you are moved to chuckle and laugh as you page through this book.

Laughter is good for your health, good for your spirit, and—as I can personally testify—good for creativity.

Ever since that moment of *deswine* inspiration when I did my first pastel pig painting in 2003, I can't get pigs out of my mind. I keep having ideas for new works faster than I can paint them.

The idea, of course, always revolves around some *double entendre*, parody, or situation made funny by replacing a human with a pig. I try to bring the work to a level of art that distinguishes it from a cartoon.

D. A. Hammond (seated) at a book signing for **Pigs ina Poke**™ **Collection #1** with publisher Brad Marion (standing).

I've been honored by all the attention my personal specialty has won me. Not only have my paintings been featured in exhibits, on television, and of course, in print, but my neighbors and friends now call me the "Pigmeister," or simply "The Pig Guy." I couldn't be more flattered.

Maybe you'll think of a new title yourself that you can share with me. After all, I'm hard at work on *COLLECTION #3*. Please write *dah@pigsinapoke.com*.

Section 1

Pigs on Vacation

Moon Over My Hami

It was beer and a game of beach volley ball. Body surfing. Another beer. Hitting on hot, scantily-clothed sows. Another beer. A swim. Yet another beer. A nap in the sun, followed by another beer. A stroll up the beach which made him thirsty for a few more beers. Then came cocktail hour. After cocktail hour, a six-pack of Hamms.

That's how poor Hami here wound up beached with the moon coming up. "Miami, you hang the moon for Hami."

Moon Over My Hami

Bay of Pigs

Everyone knows about the ill-fated Cuban invasion back in '61. What they don't know is that the same bay was taken over last year by American beach volley ball players. Here you see Misty May and Penny Will playing an exciting match.

Be careful, Piggies! Pork has been in short supply on Fidel Cochino's island for years. Misty may just wind up in a Cuban sandwich.

Bay of Pigs

Roasting Pork

On this spit of beach they start the roasting. We're talking about Heidi Hog and her friend Half-Baked Hannah. From the other white meat, they turn to pink and red and then brown. When they are finally roasted, they gather up their piglets and head home. It's all a day at the beach for these lovely mamas.

Roasting Pork

Bacon in the Sun

Pork bellies are definitely up, out and sizzling on the beaches this summer. In spite of love handles, rollovers, and sheer mass of flesh, they're dressed as skimpily as possible and slathering on Copperpig-tone by the gallon. And nothing browns up better than bacon in the pan.

What a way to relax! A colorful towel the size of a rug, a fashionable umbrella, your favorite beverage, and a little snack food... Well, lugging out the fifty-gallon cooler and several bushels of chips, pretzels, cheese and crackers was quite a sweaty task, but now we're here, without a care in the world, listening to HogTalk radio and watching the meat on parade.

The challenging thing is to fry up evenly and avoid a burn. Some porkers take this to the extreme, setting timers and repositioning the strings of what little ornamentation they're wearing to avoid tan lines. Tan lines on the butt are a difficult problem. Serious tanners use tape or clips, periodically moving them to stretch open those annoying folds of skin on the belly and hips.

A healthy glob of sunblock smeared on the snout is a good idea to protect that sensitive spot. Nothing's worse than showing up at the office with a seared schnozz.

Bacon in the Sun

Pigs in a Blanket with a Side of Mermaid

Chubs fell asleep and slipped into a dream filled with tall-masted ships adrift among distant, tropical islands. He was posted high in the crow's nest, scanning the restless horizon for the white flashes that mark hull-slashing reefs when he first spotted the mythic creatures. Some were splashing playfully in the water, their splendid hair floating in a gentle mass around them. Some were sunning themselves on the warm rocks, just above the surf line. As the ship drew nearer, he could hear their sweet voices lifted in songs of enchantment. His eyes filled with wonder as he gazed upon the beauty of their full-bodied figures, the upper torso with its sow-like features and the lower portion glittering with scales and fin.

Chubs was amazed as the creatures called him by name, beckoning for him to join them. They enticed him with sweet snorts and gentle motions of their not-so-willow-like arms. He could see they really needed the services only a real boar could provide. He was just about to leap into the water with them and swim to their palatial underwater sty where they promised to make him Head Hog and feed him dainties and delicacies from sumptuous platters.

Suddenly he woke with a start and realized that he'd tipped an iced drink into his lap as he imagined himself swinging gallantly out over the waves and letting go of a rope. The shock brought him back quickly to reality and he realized that he was not surrounded by giggling mermaids but sharing a blanket on a beach with his snoring wife.

"Humph," he snorted (but then he often used that expression).

Pigs in a Blanket with a Side of Mermaid

Section 2

Cold Ham

Hog-High on Skiing

Hog here can't wait for the après ski. He skis the foam, before he skis the powder. Before he even clamps on his boots, he has hit at least six mountains—all of them on cans of Coors. And once he's on the slopes, it's downhill from there. By midday he's skiing slalom and doesn't even know it. When it comes to athletic performance, this guy is strictly Busch league—as in Anheuser-Busch.

Hog-High on Skiing

Powder Pigs

Fresh powder! Oh boy! The powder pigs are out there first. Skiing in powder is the ultimate experience on the slopes. However, it entails certain difficulties: softer turns, and refined techniques are essential.

Skis dive in powder. This can be even more challenging if you're carrying a little extra weight from that ten course pig-out at the ski lodge last night. Make sure that your boots are not too stiff. Your skis will float if you have softer-flexing boots and there will be more room for your hoofs.

Not being able to manage both your skis can be due to your left and right hams being aligned differently. Make sure to clean off the bottom part of your boots after a crash in powder. Your skiing will be affected if you have snow packed on your equipment, especially if it's covering your visor and you can't see.

When carving a turn in powder, you need to bend both skis. But this is a hard thing to do for some skiers. It can be related to lack of proper timing and/or too many stiff drinks at last night's party. Make sure that you have skis with the right length and stiffness. If you grabbed someone else's this morning, you're in for a rough ride.

Too much thinking will land you face down in a mogul. Just watch Jean-Claude Squealie and try to act as hog-wild as he does.

Powder Pigs

Pig Out on the Slopes

This guy won a gold medal at Lillehammer. His event was the slop slalom. Buckets of slops which he had to ski around. He actually stopped and ate a bucket or two. After pigging out, the added weight gave him even more speed. That's what won him the gold.

If you think pigs don't fly, you should see this one go!

Pig Out on the Slopes

Cross-Country Trail Hog

Pigs are known for their love of winter sports. With plenty of flab, they are well insulated from the cold.

They do have limitations. Even modern technology has not yet been able to engineer a pair of snow shoes that can support 600-1200 pounds of waddling bacon without forcing a very uncomfortable bow-legged stance.

All the popular magazines are hyping up the benefits of diets and exercise. You'll see models smiling on the cover, bragging about how much weight they've lost (right next to a photo of that 1800 calorie per slice dessert that's just like the one Mama used to make). They say the motions of Nordic skiing build up muscle and reduce fat in all the right places.

Cross-country skis have been designed that are long, elegant and extra, extra, extra wide. Kick, pole, glide. Kick, pole, glide. Stop for another snack. Maybe another kick, pole, glide and it's time for lunch.

All this activity sure works up an appetite. Wasn't there some dessert in this knapsack?

Cross-Country Trail Hog

Sunrise Schussboomer

Boomer likes his liquor straight up and his skiing straight down. It's always the steepest slope for him and he's in a crouch or airborne all the way, like he's trying to outrun an avalanche. The trouble is no one had better be in front of him when he steams into the bottom and the slightest snag and he's cooked. He had an epic crash on a sunrise run he made last week that began with a scouring face plant, followed by an 80 mile per hour belly shimmy, and finishing with Boomer rolling up inside of a giant snowball. As he gradually recovered, he was greeted by ecstatic cheers from a camerapig who claimed to have caught all the drama on video.

"That was great! I'll have the whole thing on YouTuba by this evening," the documentarian promised. "You'll be famous!"

Boomer licked his wounds, gathered up what was left of his skis, found some solace and pain relievers in the lodge, and warmed up that evening at the bar. He convinced some young buck to pull up the feature on the Internet and the next thing he knew he was watching an episode titled "Abominable Snowboar Sighting at Famous Ski Resort." It showed none of the great tumbling and cascading action after Boomer careened out-of-control, but showed a beastly and vaguely porcine figure emerging slowly with truly scary groans from a snow bank and charging at the camera.

"Fifteen seconds of fame," as Andy Warthog would say.

Sunrise Schussboomer

Deviled Ham on a Plank

Yo, Dude, this ho-dad porker really has the moves. Deviled Ham here calls his board, "Underwood." He has been hogging the slopes since he was a wee piglet in his first baggy pants.

Deviled Ham is the scourge of the slopes. The nemesis of the proper downhill pigs: no manners, no class, no regrets. And after skiing, he's just as boorish.

Thank goodness no one understands his snowboard speak.

Deviled Ham on a Plank

Section 3

Pigs and Romance

Pig of My Heart

Vaudeville is not dead. Whether it's the old soft shoe or a classic song, Vaudeville Pig here really struts and sings his stuff. He knows all the oldies:

Pig of My Heart

It's a Long Way to Tip-a-piggy

Sweet Armour Ham

A Barbecue Built for Two

Shuffle Off to Omaha

Hammy, How I Love You

Pig of My Heart

Hogs and Kisses

I think that I shall never see
A sight so lovely as the swine in thee.

A pig whose hungry mouth is pressed
Against the swill trough with the best;

A pig that thinks of food all day,
And sports such hefty hams to weigh;

A pig that may in summer wear
A coat of muck in prickly hair;

Upon whose backside snow has lain;
Who seldom thinks to employ the brain.

Poems are made by fools like me,
But oh my lordy, what a pig art thee.

Hogs and Kisses

Be My Valenswine

Roses are red
Violets are blue
Sugar is sweet
And so are you.

Your eyes are like stars
They sparkle at night.
Your hair's like the ocean
With waves in the light.

You have a nice smile
You have a nice snout
But when I sniff, Babe,
I want to pass out.

Be My Valenswine

Frankly My Dear, I Don't Give a Ham!

"Frankly, my dear, I don't give a ham!" is a line from the 1939 film *Gotta Get Downwind* starring Clark Grubber and Vivien Flay-in-the mud.

It was spoken by Grubber, as Wart, in his last words to Scarlett Odorous. It occurs at the end of the film when Scarlett asks Wart, "Where shall I go? What shall I do?" if he leaves her. It demonstrates that Wart has finally given up on Scarlett ever taking a proper bath and no longer cares what happens to her.

The famous film, shot in Technicolor, is pigema's greatest, bacon-studded, epic film of the Old South during wartime that boasts an immortal cast in a timeless, classic tale of a love-hate romance. The heroine, Scarlett Odorous, struggles to find love during the years between baths and ultimately must seek refuge for herself and her family back at the beloved There-Ah! sty. She defends her pen against other sows, freeloaders, and starvation itself. She finally marries her worldly admirer, Wart Blusterer, but her apathy toward bathing dooms their battling relationship, and she again returns to There-Ah! to find consolation—in spite of her odor.

A well-publicized casting search for an actress to play the Southern sow Scarlett resulted in the hiring of young British actress Vivien Flay-in-the mud, although over thirty other actresses applied for the heavyweight role.

Frankly My Dear, I Don't Give a Ham!

Bringing Home the Bacon

The average gestation period for sows is 114 days (less than 4 months). The most critical period in the life cycle of a pig is from birth to weaning. On the average, about two pigs per litter are lost during this period. Sows used to be quarantined to a farrowing house to get extra care during this time, but now it's more common for them to make several trips to the hogspital for regular prenatal examinations by the Gyne-hog-alist.

The hogspital has special facilities set up for the actual delivery, with music, dimmed lights, warm bath, and, of course, cameras rolling and a whole retinue of commentators to witness the births and count the pink piglets as they drop. "One, two, three..." Since the average litter is ten to twelve (large litters of 25 or more are possible) with a 15-20 minute interval between each piglet birth, the count is rarely finished accurately. The unruly mob of gawkers finds their interest being drawn toward the adjoining room where a feast has been spread out on long tables. As with most swine gatherings, this one rapidly transforms into a prodigious party.

Bringing Home the Bacon

Swine Lake

No one knows how Swan Lake (known locally as Swine Lake) got its name. More swamp than pond (and hardly a lake), the only "swans" that seem to stay around are actually clunky wooden paddle boats that are impossible to steer. Still the oversize Cygnets are wildly popular with middle-aged couples who frequent the dockside attraction, a family restaurant that features an all-you-can-eat buffet brunch on Sunday mornings that draws in all the local porkers.

The Trough has a tradition that cleverly avoids long lines at the door. If you have to wait for an open table, they put you out on one of the paddle boats. When someone leaves the chow-down, they holler out "all-ee, all-ee, in free" and there is a great, tumultuous churning and mini-naval battles as the swine in the boats struggle to maneuver their crafts close enough so that they can be the first hoof to touch the dock and thereby claim the table. It's actually great entertainment if you like to elbow and shove your neighbors for some genuine home cookin' or just appreciate general commotion and uproar.

Swine Lake

Section 4

Pigs at Work

Porktologist

Dr. Boarus T. Rumpus is an eminent physician specializing in a certain part of the porcine anatomy. He recently gave an address to a joint meeting of the American Medical Institute and the American Hog Institute from which we have taken the following excerpt:

> The stomach of domestic pigs is much larger than that of humans. This is probably partly due to the larger body size, but also may be partly attributed to high dietary intake. Although officially omnivorous, pigs eat mostly junk food and, as a result, the gastric chamber is somewhat modified. For example, there is a diverticulum or pouch at the top of the stomach which is probably a site for microbial metabolism...

Why was Dr. Rumpus talking about stomachs when the other end of the digestive track is supposed to be his specialty? He explains, "I've always enjoyed poking around and even though it's not directly in my field, I've had a personal interest in my own belly since I was a piglet. Besides, I figure it's got to affect what goes on downstream, if in no other way than regulating the sheer quantity of what we're dealing with."

Porktologist

Capitalist Pig

The concept of greed may be genetically encoded in some of us, but the refinements involved in thoroughly fleecing a group of trusting investors involve skills, practice, planning and dedication. Fortunately, Howie L. Cheatem, head hog at the powerful brokerage house, Bilk, Bamboozle, and Bleed, LLC, has been at it for years.

"There's always so much hype about the latest pyramid scheme," he mutters through his cigar. "There's a very simple rule you need to keep in mind when planning your financial strategy: give your money to someone and they're gonna take some of it. Hey, that's capitalism! You think we're in this for the fun of it? We're here to make money."

Howie thinks hogs are ideally suited for the crowded, stressful environs of the Stock Exchange floor. "I ain't got no use for any of them MBA types from some highbrow business school. My best traders come straight out of pig barns where they've learned basic survival skills. It's crowded, it's messy, it's loud, it smells bad—so what's the big deal? We're used to it."

Howie has this to say about the public perception that the financial system is corrupt. "Sure, I know, they think it stinks! Well, let me tell you something. Take a Ben Franklin [that's a hundred dollar bill] out on the street there and hand it to the first ham you meet. Do you think he's gonna sniff it and ask probing questions? No, he's gonna stuff it in his pocket. Folks don't care where their money comes from, long as they have some."

Capitalist Pig

Head Hog (Harry S. Trueham)

Hail to the Chief! Head Hog here has made it to the top. He was formerly a senator who was famous for his pork barrel legislation. Head Hog coined the phrases: "The swill stops here" and "If you don't like the heat, get off the spit."

Here he sits in the Oval Sty, heading the Pig Republic. It's anyone's guess to whom he is speaking. Note the portrait in the background of the celebrated patriot, Alexander *Ham*-ilton.

Head Hog (Harry S. Trueham)

Pork Moo-Shoe

Until she studied cooking in Europe after WWII, Julia Porker had no idea what to do in a kitchen. Recently released CIA documents have revealed that she worked for the U.S. spy agency for years and was sent overseas to Ceylon and Kunming, China. Julia, having top security clearances, knew every secret message that passed through her office, though she didn't always understand things clearly. For example, her first attempt to prepare moo-shoe to impress her fiancé, Paul, was a complete disaster.

Julia had a high-pitched, squeaky voice and unique mannerisms. Much of her activities around the kitchen centered around a wine bottle that was always prominently placed on the counter. Julia had not yet written down any recipes and fancied that she could reproduce entrees she'd sampled at cheap local restaurants from memory. Perhaps the wine affected her recall or perhaps war-time rationing had resulted in some significant substitutions for traditional ingredients, but years later her husband could still recollect the experience.

"It tasted like shoe leather. I thought she was trying to kill me," he says.

Paul was assigned with the U.S. Information Agency in France in 1948, and insisted that his wife get some basic cooking lessons and learn to use recipes. The couple also always ate out when they were going Chinese. Her cooking career has a place in American history, as many remember her as an enthusiastic and opinionated chef who sampled copiously as she went about her preparations from both the bottle and from the ingredients. With her many television series and cookbooks, including *SWILLING WITH JULIA*, her legacy still lives on to this day.

Pork Moo-Shoe

Pig Farmer

This pig farmer raises vegetable. Lots of them. Carrots and peas and potatoes and corn and squash and other things that don't "oink" or "moo" or go "baa."

Pigs have a affection for turning over the ground, the rich smells of the soil, the abundance of nature's bounty. Even though so many swine have been herded into the close confines of the city and spend dust-to-dawn in the tiny closets allotted to them for office space, a hog never feels better or more natural then when he or she is out in the open air with the great expanse of sky overhead, listening to the sound of corn growing on a hot July day.

Well, actually there is one thing better: eating out in the open air with a great expanse of food spread out on long tables for county fairs, barn raisings, harvest days, hay days, family reunions, birthdays, Bar Mitzvahs, Mother's Day, Father's Day, Sunday brunch, and general kick-back and take-it-easy days.

There's a lot of work involved in keeping up an agrarian lifestyle.

Pig Farmer

A Porker in a Fokker

Baron von Richthoggen here was a top German ace during The Pig War. In fact, he had about as many kills as a Chicago slaughter yard at Easter time. No wonder he earned the nickname, "The Bloody Red Deviled Ham Baron."

Here he flies over no man's land, making a veritable charcuterie of the French biplanes. Sadly for von Richthoggen, the Yanks are about to enter the war.

This proud Westphalian ham will soon be smoked by the great American ace, Eddie Hamhocker.

A Porker in a Fokker

Telling a Scary Pig Tale

The little piggies are out on their first overnight. Of course, Troop leader, Harry Boar, has an especially scary story to tell them so that they will have nightmares for a week and many of them will never be able to be out in the woods after dark, even as adult hogs, without a flashlight and a weapon close at hand. He had a way of leaning close to the fire so that the flash of flame and dancing shadows made it look like he could be a fearsome outlaw himself.

> Dirty Harry was a killer who could sneak up behind his victim in the dark as silent as a spider. His favorite weapon was a rope—just like this one—that he could sling around the neck and pull tight so fast and so hard that not the teensiest squeal would escape. The innocent piglet—just your size—would kick and wriggle, its eyes would bulge out big, and it would want to slip away and trot to its mommy sow so badly. But it was no use.
>
> Dirty Harry was very cunning and very thorough. He didn't like to leave anyone around to tell the tale. First he'd slip into one tent (one little piggy, two little piggies), then he'd slip into the next, (three little piggies, four little piggies), and then…

And then, of course, he'd send them off to bed.

"Sweet dreams," he'd snirtle. "I'll just keep this rope out here with me. Don't worry about the campfire. I'll put it out. I want to make sure it's dark and quiet so you can all get a good night's rest."

Telling a Scary Pig Tale

Professor of Pig Latin

Pig Latin 101:

Take the first consonant off the word. Don't throw it away. You'll need it later.

What if there is no consonant? You're getting ahead of me. I'll come back to that later.

Okay. So now you've got a word that starts with a vowel. Does everybody have a word that starts with a vowel? How about I give you an example so that we're all using the same word. Let's take "intelligence." No, wait, that starts with an "i." I've already told you that we want a word that starts with a consonant. What do you mean, I didn't? Okay, so I'm telling you now. We want a word that starts with a consonant, because we need a consonant to throw away. Like I said, we're not really going to throw it away. Of course, we'd never do that. We're just going to recycle it—you know, like you might recycle a beer bottle. But no, you don't get a nickel for it. That would be great if every time you spoke a word in Pig Latin you got a nickel. That would get a lot more students coming to take my class. Some of the more enterprising ones might earn their tuition, or at least beer money, that way. Of course, you wouldn't actually get a nickel for every word you spoke in Pig Latin. Why not? Use your intelligence; some words don't start with consonants. You're right, I told you not to use intelligence. That should be easy for some of you (snort, snort, chortle, chortle).

Let's take a banana. No, I don't want you to steal a banana. No, I don't want you to peel a banana. I'm talking about the word "banana," not something you eat. Let's take the "b" and recycle it. I'm not talking about an insect. No, the letter "b." Can anyone explain to the class, why the letter "b"? No one? Because it's the first letter of the word "banana." And its a consonant. And...

The bell rings and the classroom empties immediately. It's lunch time so everyone has one thing on their mind. Poor Professor Hammond didn't get too far with his lesson today. It's going to be a long semester.

Professor of Pig Latin

Section 5

Pigs and Sports

White Pigs Can't Jump

"Reach for the sky! Reach for the sky!" Billy Whitey exclaims, while barely lifting his hoofs off the floor.

He's playing the chump again, in pick-up games in the barnyard, where, because of his pale complexion, no one takes him for much of an athlete. But Billy's really out to hustle the homeboys for a few bucks out of the trough: when it comes to hoops, he's got the moves; when it comes to shooting, he's got the touch.

He dribbles. He drools. He draws fouls and he smells foul. Everything he does is just short of Magic.

Eventually Whitey gains the respect of a sharp-tongued Jimmy Dean and pairs up with him to take on the tougher sections in the 'hood. Jimmy snipes at Billy's mother, his girlfriend, his intellect, as well as his game, but his banter can carry a universal message, at least for pigs, as in the following memorable quote:

"Ya see, homey, you either smoke or you get smoked."

Even though Billy has learned to be thick-skinned, he takes genuine offense at Jimmy's sarcastic claim that "white pigs can't jump" and loses a bet to Dean by failing to slam dunk in three tries. When it comes to the real game, however, Whitey has an uncanny ability to put himself "in the zone" and comes through in the final seconds of the big one, when Jimmy lobs an "alley-oop" over the rim and Billy stuffs it.

White Pigs Can't Jump

Bird Pig on Point

It was a strange field trial, indeed. Bob D'Auria's Elhew pointer, Beau, was a shoe-in for first place. Five finds in as many minutes. Perfect high tail and intense point. Steady as a rock, when the birds flushed and the guns went off.

That was before Farmer Farnum's broody sow, Emma, got out of her sty. Poor old gal wandered off and got lost. Emma went searching for her piglets and came upon a covey of quail. She went on point. Perfect high corkscrew tail. Right front trotter raised in a classic point.

Then, she did something no bird dog judge has ever seen. Emma plopped down on her fat side and suckled the entire covey of quail.

Bird Pig on Point

Hoggis MacDuff

Hoggis is from a long line of duffers. His Dad placed golf balls in his crib and looked on with admiration whenever he saw his son gnawing on them. "When he gets down to the rubber band part, he'll get a deeper understanding of the sport," he said.

The local course is quite a challenge. There are high winds, narrow fairways, tiny greens, wicked sand traps, and a pervasive dampness from the sea. Hoggis has learned to compensate for much of this by banging his club against a rock anytime one of his shots sails off course and lands in the drink. Although his club shafts and heads are now bent at many weird angles, his shots tend to veer off the tee at an incredible angle only to curve back towards the flag as if drawn by a magnet. American players, with all their fancy equipment have never been able to imitate his successful style.

There's one thing, though, Hoggis has never found a solution to: those high winds. They blow up his leg, freeze his knees and occasionally lift his kilt, which leads Hoggis to use an unpleasant expletive.

"Ballocks," he exclaims.

Hoggis MacDuff

Minnesota Fats

Minnesota Fats was saved from a short career at the Hormel packing plant by a pool cue. He grew up in a Pool Sty and learned to hustle pool as a wee piglet.

Minnesota Fats once ran twelve straight tables, including two buffet tables and one entire smorgasbord.

Whatever you do, don't wager with this guy. He'll set you up with a few slop shots and pretend it's beginner's luck. Then he'll innocently suggest a little wager. "Just to make it more interesting."

That's when you want to leave or he'll be the one bringing home the bacon.

Minnesota Fats

Pig Out at Home

Every other Sunday, the home team hosts a baseball game followed by a picnic. The whole town turns out—for the picnic, which is quite the spread. The ball game is played according to some rather eclectic rules. There are only three innings and each player is only allowed to bat once. Also it's slow-pitch, so everyone gets a chance to hit and run. The runner has to be tagged out. There are no forced outs. And the inning doesn't end with the third out; any runners left on base have a chance to book it for home.

The rules make for some interesting situations, especially since some of the runners are harder to catch than a greased pig. The outfielders tend to drift off early, as the aromas from the barbecue pits become too powerful to resist, so any ball that gets through the infield is likely to result in a score. The most valuable player tends to be the catcher, who has to stay for the final out—or the final play at home. There aren't many disputed plays; in fact, often no one can really remember the final score. But everyone in town reviews the merits, quantities, and presentation of each dish served up at the picnic, with comments on who made the big play for the last sandwich, drumstick, or deep dish Dutch apple pie.

Yes, that's right, someone was such a pig that they snorted down the whole pie.

Pig Out at Home

Salt Pork

Salt Pork has spent so much time at sea that he has salt water in his veins. When it comes to sailing, he has done it all: the America's Cup, the TransPac, the Bermuda Race, the Iowa Farm Pond…

Saltie can "oink up" a change in the wind and "squeal down" a Nor'easter. And when it comes to sailing, he has no equal. As for navigation, he's the greatest navigator since Captain James Fully-Cooked.

Salt Pork

Section 6

Pigs and Pop Culture

You Ain't Nothin' But a Round Hog

Elvis impersonators are incredibly popular among pigs. The hip swaying motion just seems to come natural to them and if pigs were born with sideburns, you'd swear there was a family resemblance.

The King had many titles that were meant to appeal to the porkers that his agents told him made up a major portion of his fans.

Blue Suede Hooves
Pork Salad Annie
A Big Hunk o' Pork
All Shook Up (Are We Having Baked Pork Chops Tonight?)
Don't Be Cruel, I'd Like Seconds Too
Are You Lonesome Tonight, Sooey

Of course, there's nothing more moving than the words to this song:

You ain't nothin' but a round hog
Squealin' all the time.
You ain't nothin' but a round hog
Squealin' all the time.
Well, you ain't never et six pizzas
And you ain't no friend of mine.

When they said you was a huge one,
Well, that was just a lie.
When they said you was a huge one,
Well, that was just a lie.
You ain't never et six pizzas
And you ain't no friend of mine

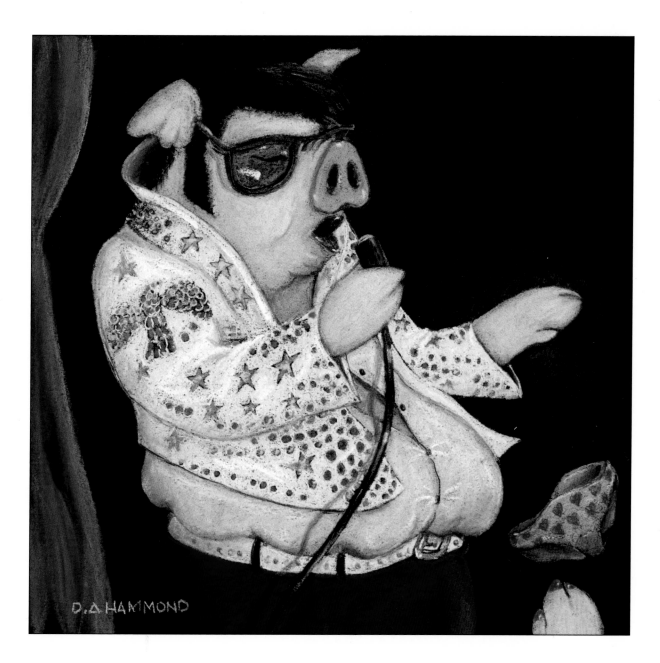

You Ain't Nothin' But a Round Hog

Play It Again, Ham

"Yeah," he snorts, "you sang it for her and you're gonna sing it for me. If she can stand it, I can!"
So Ham bangs it out:

>You must remember this
>A snort is just a snort, a grunt is just a grunt.
>The fundamental things apply
>As hooves go by.
>
>And when two piggies woo
>They still say, "I love food, too."
>On that you can rely
>No matter what the future brings
>As hooves go by.
>
>Moonlight and shared swill
>Never out of date.
>Stomachs need to be filled
>Eating early and late.
>Sows need the boar
>A boar must have his mate
>That no one can deny.
>
>It's still the same old story
>A fight for love and gorging
>A case of do or die.
>The world will always welcome piggies
>As hooves go by.
>
>Oh yes, the world will always welcome piggies
>As hooves go by.

Play It Again, Ham

Ellen the Generous Does Her Pig Jig

The Pig Meister has a few pointers for those talk show hosts who like to come out dancing at the start of their program:

Listen, Ellen, this is the pig jig.
You've gotta have rhythm. You've gotta have beat.
You've gotta always act light on your feet.

You're gonna rout with you nose
You're gonna sniff in the air
Then turn it around
And wiggle your derrière.

Ellen the Generous Does Her Pig Jig

Happy Quilting Bee Sowciety

Quilt making among porcine groups is big business. That is, the quilts must be of an extraordinary size to be large enough to offer full comfort.

It may be stating the obvious, but when you put a tape measure to one of those grumpy old boars, it had better be a long one. What you really need to take into consideration, though, is how notorious they are for hogging all the covers on their side of the stall.

So why are these sows so happy? They just discovered that certain patterns attract bees, especially a particularly nasty sort that's newly arrived from South America. This insect, being Amazonian, is not overly fond of males to begin with, but something about the vibrations a big bad boar puts out when he's snoring just drive it crazy. They think that it's the buzzing of a rival hive and they gather in a huge cloud of swirling stingers and head straight for the snout emanating the horrid snorts, wheezes and chortles.

Once the commotion dies down, the boar usually goes to look for some mud to rout around in to soothe the pain, leaving the quilt to the other occupant.

The gals are looking forward to a little fun and the best night's sleep they've had in years.

Happy Quilting Bee Sowciety

Charlie Porkski

Charlie Porkski is the greatest comedian in Poland.

Once asked, "Charlie, I understand you are the greatest comedian in Poland. To what do you attribute your succ—"

Charlie interrupted, "Timing!"

He really Krakows them up over there!

Charlie used to tell long, sophisticated stories with satirical twists that would elicit groans when he delivered the punch line. Then he discovered that he could still get groans even when he shortened his tales. Sometimes his mere entry into the room could produce groans—even snarls. So now Charlie sticks pretty much to one-liners. Some of his classics are:

- Support bacteria—they're the only culture some swine have.
- Never wrestle with a pig—you'll both get dirty and the pig will like it.
- At the feed trough, the only substitute for good manners is fast reflexes.
- Never try to reason with a pig. It's a waste of time and it annoys the pig.
- My mind is like a steel trap—rusty and illegal in 37 states.
- Talking about pork…despite the cost of living, have you noticed how popular it remains?
- I just got lost in thought, and it was unfamiliar territory.
- Am I ambivalent? Well, yes and no.
- In an argument, a sow always has the last word. Anything a boar says after that is the beginning of a new argument.
- If you're riding ahead of the drove, take a look back every now and then to make sure it's still there.
- I had amnesia once—maybe twice.
- Take my sweet wife—please!

Bada-bing, bada-bing, bada-boom!

Charlie Porkski, the Polish Ham

On Porky, On Hammy...

Forget about eight tiny reindeer. Santa Hog uses small pigs to deliver the Yuletide goodies. Presents for good little piglets all over the world. And because sties have no roofs, he can park right on the side. Good thing, because Santa Hog can no longer fit down a chimney.

After Santa Hog makes a delivery you can hear him cry as he roars out of sight: "On Hammy, on Grunter, on Sausage and Scrapple; On Fat Back, Side Pork, Cracklin'...and Lead Pig with the Apple!" Of course, that's not their real names, but Santa's job is hard work and he get's distracted thinking about the big feast he's going to dig in to once he returns to his cozy place at the North Pole.

On Porky, On Hammy, On Moo Shoe, On Bacon and
Hogen das, On Pigalo and Squealy, On Grunter...

Section 7

Barnyard Humor

OK, Who Farted?

One of the hazards of any pig gathering is flatulence. After all, if you eat garbage, what do you expect?

There's always one pig who "cuts the slops." See if you can guess the culprit? Pig on lower right appears to be very proud of himself. And how 'bout the white faced one playing possum? Or it could be the second from the left with the sly expression on his kisser. Then again, the one third from left looks way too innocent...

Answer: Pig at top. He who calls it generally owns it.

OK, Who Farted?

Pigs Happen!

It's not the stork who delivers fresh little piglet trotters into the world. But sometimes the family tree can get a little difficult to trace for more than a generation or two. Pigs tend to be populists and don't act snooty about pedigree.

"It is a wise pig who knows his own father," as The Great Lard, Shakespig, said (or perhaps that was said by Sir Francis Bacon—anyhow, someone said it).

Perhaps the little piglet in the foreground gives us an insight into the genetic strain. But here is a thought on tolerance and diversity: once we've rolled in the mud, we all look the same.

Pigs Happen!

Say Again, It's a Flying WHAT?

CROW 1 TO CROW 2: "What is that?"

CROW 2: "Looks like a pig roosting in a tree."

CROW 1: "But how…?"

CROW 2: "By flapping those silly looking wings?"

CROW 1: "It doesn't take a degree in aerodynamics to see that those little wings would never get that much bacon off the ground."

A blast of fire startles the two birds and another pig roosts nearby.

PIG 1 TO PIG 2: "Aren't crows the most annoying birds?"

PIG 2: "Always acting like such know-it-alls."

PIG 1: "Do you think anything with a brain the size of a pea will ever understand jet propulsion?"

PIG 2: (Blasting off with another mighty fart.) "When crows turn white!"

Say Again, It's a Flying WHAT?

Happy as a Pig in Shitakes

Don't "truffle" with this porker! He is an expert at sniffing out mushrooms. His mother, after all, was a champion (or is it champignon?) French Truffle Pig.

There's nothing this guy likes more than to go into the woods in search of fungi. Morels will make him giddy. Criminis will make him laugh. Portobellos will have his fat sides shaking with mirth. But he is never happier than when he is knee deep in Shitakes.

Happy as a Pig in Shitakes

Hog-Powered Hybrid

Who needs BP when you've got your own gas? And pigs have plenty of gas. They call it methane. This six-cylinder hybrid truck runs entirely on porcine flatulence. It burns cleanly and makes America free from dependence on foreign oil. Most of those OPEC bigwigs don't like pigs anyway.

As for mileage, the little truck here is incredible. It gets an amazing twelve miles per fart.

Hog-Powered Hybrid

Pull My Hoof

Whew! Where there's gas, there's fire!

Every boar seems to love to play the "pull my hoof" game. While there are those who consider the practice to be vulgar, they obviously do not appreciate that proper execution requires a sense of timing, discreteness (waiting until the Sow is not around), and performance skills.

Porky was first introduced to the game last week by his uncle. You should have seen his reaction. This particular joke was beyond hilarious to him. He actually fell to the floor and wiggled his toes in the air, he was laughing so hard.

Proud of his well executed expulsion of flatulence, the old boar didn't realize the pungent set of events that he'd set in motion.

It wasn't long after this that Porky came bouncing up to him, foreleg extended, giggling so hard that he could hardly stand. "Pull my hoof, pull my hoof!"

Imitation is the highest form of flattery. The proud boar reached down and pulled Porky's primary toe. Slowly the little oinker's cute smile turned into something more of a grimace. His beady eyes narrowed and a pink blush and look of intense concentration spread across his face. After a few silent seconds, he gave up and announced that "it didn't work."

He was obviously disappointed. His mother had rushed forward, so a lesson in technique was not possible at that moment.

A little later, a stain appeared on the backside of Porky's pajamas. It was suspiciously skid-mark in nature. The poor piglet had learned how *not* to do the "pull my hoof" trick!

Pull My Hoof

Section 8

Pigs of Dubious Taste

Napoleham

Born in a simple sty in Corsica, Nebraska, young Napoleham went on to become Porcine Emperor of the Midwest. He rose to power quickly in the fattening pens of Nebraska. His early victories were fabled. Unfortunately he bit off more than he could chew. After an ill fated invasion of Moscow, Kansas, he was exiled to Elba, Missouri. He did make a brief comeback, however.

Everyone knows of his final and tragic defeat at Waterloo, Iowa.

Napoleham

Pigasus

The circumstances surrounding the birth of Pigasus are still unclear. Some say that he was put on earth by Athena after the famous winged horse Pegasus was elevated to the heavens by Zeus and made a constellation. (This seems most unlikely, but the nice thing about myths is that anything can happen.)

The hero Bellerophon had easily tamed Pegasus by walking up to him with a golden bridle that Athena had supplied. This annoyed Zeus who had previously used the horse to lug around a supply of lightning bolts. It didn't take Zeus long to get even with Bellerophon (with the old gadfly trick).

In the meantime, though, Athena had created a new job for Pegasus, delivering messages from the Muses to poets. (Wow! An early air mail system—those Greeks were sure inventive.)

Of course, after Pegasus got elevated to the Hall of Fame, the Muses were reluctant to go back to snail mail. They tried pony express for a mile, but it just didn't cut it. After a lot of angry odes started being written trashing Olympus, Athena was able to convince Zeus to let her use a flying pig.

"No would-be hero is going to be caught dead flying around on a winged pig," she argued convincingly.

And no poet's ever going to admit to seeing the messenger, she thought, impressed by the cleverness of her own solution.

Pigasus

Oui, Oui, Oui, All the Way Home

Zees little piggy went to Les Halles market.

Zees little piggy stayed *à maison.*

Zees little piggy had *Rôti de boeuf à la sauce Bordelaise.*

And zees little piggy had three liters of vin ordinaire, several beers, two cognacs and a tumbler of absinthe.

Little wonder he went *Oui, Oui,* Wee all the way home

Oui, Oui, Oui, All the Way Home

Nocturnal Food Hog

In the wee, wee, wee hours of the morning, you can find him. His fat hocks silhouetted by the moon and his pork belly illuminated by the refrigerator light. It's Nocturnal Food Hog. He's up for his third "midnight snack." He's all alone—just as well that no one has to suffer his boarish table (or refrigerator shelf) manners.

Then it's back to bed, to rest up for breakfast. Or perhaps one more midnight snack…

Nocturnal Food Hog

Pork Pius the First with His Cardinal

Ever hear of Vaticanned Ham? Pork Pius I is it. Not to pontificate, but Pius is God's infallible intermediary here on earth. And is he ever busy!

Making Papal Bulls (He prefers to call them Papal Boars). Dressing up in nifty robes. Cleaning up messes left in holy sties around the globe.

Pork Pius I's one great relaxation is his pet Cardinal. The bird's name is Bernard. Pius loves playing with Bernard. Kissing his little beak. Singing him Gregorian chants. Giving him Papal blessings. The two are inseparable.

Pork Pius the First with His Cardinal

Deviled Ham and Eggs

Diablo Jamón used to have a problem with his sty mates stealing his food. Not any more. DJ's mastered the art of cooking with hot sauce and developed a taste for spices that bring flames to the mouth, heavy sweats to the brow, and double the pulse rate—and that's just the first spoonful. Someone once challenged DJ to a hot food eating contest. Once.

The smell of those ripe habeneras DJ uses is so strong, it sends would-be visitors howling back home before they even get halfway up the walk to the door. Although his breath can set off a smoke alarm, Jamón has a discriminatory palate. He can deliver grand orations on the subtle differences in pungency produced by the capsaicin in various chili pepper seeds, (if you tried even a nibble you'd probably find your vocabulary reduced to strained syllables that resemble "wa—ter!") But DJ is not without compassion. He stores rolls of toilet paper in his freezer to hand out to dinner guests before they leave, reminding them that the delights of the evening will be felt again since the "ring of fire" always "burns twice."

Deviled Ham and Eggs

Pigs of a Feather Flock Together

Birds of a feather flock together means that people who have common interests often spend time together.

Example: "Those guys work at the same funeral home and go to the same bars. They do everything together."

Reply: "Birds of a feather flock together."

We know birds are of the same type when they have the same feathers; they are "of a feather." When birds join together in groups with other birds they are known as a flock. Just as birds often flock with other birds of the same "feather," so do people who are like each other spend time together.

Example: "Are Porky and his friends going to that same bar again?"

Reply: "Sure they are. Birds of a feather flock together."

Pigs who are similar to each other and share the same interests (of a feather) often spend time with each other (flock together).

Example: "Look. The whole sty is shouldering their way up to the trough at the same time, as always."

Reply: "Pigs of a feather flock together."

Pigs of a Feather Flock Together

About the Authors and More about Pigs in a Poke™

Duane Hammond, aka D. A. Hammond, is a Buckingham Scholarship graduate from the Museum School of Fine Arts, Boston, Massachusetts (1964).

Immediately after graduation, until 1969, he worked as a graphic designer and art director for advertising agencies in New Hampshire and Boston.

In 1969 he started his own graphic design company, The Magnificent Art Machine, and in 1981 the name was changed to Hammond Design Associates, Inc. For thirty-nine years, Duane produced award-winning sales and marketing literature and advertising materials for many businesses. Some of his national and multi-national clients included EG & G, Inc., Data General, Bell & Howell, Sylvania and Compaq, plus manufacturers, financial institutions and non-profit organizations.

He has won many awards for his design including two NH Graniteer Best of Show Awards, Hatch Awards, Boston and New York Art Directors Awards, Desi Awards and over thirty-five more from other recognized trade groups. He has also had his work published in such prestigious magazines as PRINT and CA.

Now semi-retired, Duane spends his time painting pastels and watercolors. He has won several awards for his work and his paintings are on exhibit and for sale throughout New Hampshire in many galleries.

Duane is a member of the New Hampshire Artists Association, Governor Wentworth Art association, and the Manchester Art Association.

His painting style includes impressionism and realism. Subjects range from seascapes, landscapes and cityscapes to wildlife and a series of whimsical, satirical pigs.

Lawrence K. DeLamarter is the owner of DeLamarter Advertising Services, Inc. in Concord, Massachusetts. He is on the faculty at Boston University as a lecturer in the Communications department, teaching primarily Advertising. He received his B.A. from the

The three pigs in the barnyard: Duane, Larry, and Brad.

University of Colorado; M.A., Universidad de las Americas (Mexico). He is an avid golfer, (when he plays golf), fisherman, hunter and outdoorsman.

Bradley Marion is the publisher of Beech River Books. He received his B.A. from Belknap College, Center Harbor, N.H. and M.Ed. from Plymouth State University in Plymouth, N.H. He is the author of three books of poetry and teaches in the field of Special Education with challenged adolescents. His wife, Dawn, is an oil painter and illustrator and their son, Ethan, is a graphic artist.

Pigs ina Poke™ is a wonderful collection of satirical and whimsical pigs in artwork created since 2003 by D. A. Hammond. You can go on-line to *http://www.pigsinapoke.com* and you'll see links to all kinds of wonderful **Pigs ina Poke**™ pigphenalia such as cards, magnets and framable quality prints. We keep adding to the list of artwork and reproductions, so check in periodically.

And soon there will be Collection #3… After suffering through some of our puns, you may have a good idea of your own you'd like to share with us, so please e-mail us at *dah@pigsinapoke.com*.

The End, Butt...

Look for Collection #3, (Coming Soon!)